Love's
Light

DANA NICOLE HALEY

Balboa Press books may be ordered through booksellers or by contacting:

Balboa Press
A Division of Hay House
1663 Liberty Drive
Bloomington, IN 47403
www.balboapress.com
1 (877) 407-4847

ISBN: 978-1-5043-5050-1 (sc)
ISBN: 978-1-5043-5051-8 (e)

Library of Congress Control Number: 2016902520

Print information available on the last page.

Balboa Press rev. date: 09/15/2016

BALBOA
PRESS
A DIVISION OF HAY HOUSE

For Temple of Peace Healing Sanctuary & Awakening

In Paradise Maui friends who completely enlightened

my life, my wonderfully supportive parents, and

Steven Eaton, who funded this project & continued

to believe in me through it all.

Foreword

In my twenties, I tried to meditate, but was distracted by my own thoughts and external noises. After many years of hearing about the benefits of meditation, I attempted to meditate again. Knowing what I was in for, I decided I had no choice but to relax and, instead of trying to block the noises that distracted me, go ahead and give them my full attention.

Any emotional resistance I felt towards any noise took a direct, dark path from my body and into the ground as I focused on appreciating all that touched my ears. Sitting with my eyes shut, observing and identifying each sound, a wave of acceptance washed through me. They weren't nearly as bad when I wasn't trying to block them out!

I listened intently until they began to fragment like a Jackson Pollock painting. Mother Earth had absorbed and swallowed the irritation I felt. I still felt resistance to something, but it wasn't the noise. I felt my eyes fill with tears that spilled down my face as I let uncategorized sadness flow from me.

Like a wave rising up to well my eyes and flow down onto my cheeks, I opened depths of leagues of emotions until my well ran dry. As it arose, I again let it go; all drama delivered into terra's filtering fertility.

A pure resonance of peace began to fill me as I imagined a large stream of white light pouring into my head, pushed by a pulse through my mind. It filtered through me, from the top down, with each beat of my heart. I listened to the abstract, fragmented scene of every playing child's shriek, car's alarm, and dog's bark. They blended into one sequence of acceptance.

I slipped into a daydream. White light surrounded me while angels floated behind me, touching my shoulders. The sensation of their touch sent tingles through my whole body. I floated there in my fantasy, marveling at the feelings of absolute peace and love that filled me.

I felt myself start to slip back into a concern; I don't remember what it was. All I knew is that I didn't want the darkness I'd released to shadow my being again, so I asked the angels, "How can I stay in the light?"

An immediate response echoed behind my ears and resonated through my head. The angels reassured me that they would always be there; that I could always rely on them. Then came the overwhelming feeling of being rocked, cradled, and completely embraced by the most "everything is wonderful, everything is perfect, and love is all there is" feeling I've ever experienced.

The reassurance they gave me - that everything would be okay no matter what happens in this physical life - was completely game changing for me. It was the reminder I needed that I was on the right track in life. It reaffirmed my spirituality, and that brought me great hope.

I decided I wanted to share that hope with the world. I meditated again and listened for the answers to my concerns. I asked, "What should I do to bring love and light messages to the world?"

"Write a book," they responded.

"How will I know what to write?" I hadn't the foggiest idea of where to begin.

"We will tell you."

Wow: They would tell me what to write! All I had to do was meditate and listen to the answers from the angels! They made me feel so cradled, comforted, calm, and okay with everything that I knew I would not fail. I had found a new, exciting purpose to fulfill: To spread the messages I received from the angels with the world.

When I began my mission, the words of the angels gushed through me like a river flowing in a spring snow melt! They popped into head so fast, and sometimes all at once! To solve this, I started recording myself repeating aloud what they were telling me, and thus began this angel-inspired adventure into Love's Light.

Six months into writing, I decided I wanted to give my audience the *experience* of feeling Love's Light. This idea went beyond that which I had painted with words: I wanted the immediacy and the unspoken thousand words a picture could portray.

The photos in this book were taken on the many trails I've traveled in the past five years or so. I have always enjoyed making fun out of exercise by snapping photos when I go for a walk. These photos represent just a dash of the beauty I found in Maui, Oahu, Washington State, Idaho, and Northern California.

In the midst of a major metropolitan area, right next to the freeway's onramp, or in the middle of the center divider of a busy thoroughfare: Gorgeous buds no one seemed to notice as they whizzed by bloomed, saying "You can't erase Love's Light, we flowers will never let you!"

Wishing you much compassion and joy for your journey,

Dana

Love's Light

Look! I'm alive! Moving and changing
Breathing with waves and wind; existing
Feeling and being a love light
Being and feeling the love of life

Abundantly flying through ecstasy
Pollen awaiting this drunken bee
Being, creating beautiful sweets
Art, laughter, and smiling babies

Promoting life; God is seen
Amidst all faiths and upbringings
All love and light exist right now
All lost thought is nothing but found

Life exists because of no one
We exist because of everyone
Joyfully cruising through this life
Happily glowing in love's light

Spark

We give ourselves
The ability to become superstars but
When determination is discovered
In the wishes of others we
Become overwhelmed

We need to fan our own fire,
We know the flame is in there
Feeling the perfect moment
To spark

(Let it happen now)

Love's Grace

Beautiful light, balancing dark
In love with life, down at the park
You are the blossoms, cherries and blues
On all the branches, and we are all you

In this infinite lifetime, not far behind us
In our view, here and now are all we do
There is no bad, there is only good
The earth and the sea tremble as they should

We are together, everything one
Spinning and twirling under the sun
The feeling of living is the feeling of loving
Abundantly sharing; we're one in love

Love's grace defines us
And nothing divides us
Love's grace defines us
And nothing divides us

Divine Love

Love is here for me
Love is here for you
When we listen closely
We know just what to do

Sit back and shut our eyes
Listen to our breathing sighs
Listen to the birds sing
Take in all the beauty

And let one love guide us
Our deepest instincts find us
Divine love rests inside us, guiding us
Doesn't it feel good?

So much joy we bring to all
When we dance and sing our unique song
Letting the world know
We've got so much good to show!

Beauty is abounding
When everyone is laughing
Loving each and everyone
Each and everyone being love

When love grows and we show it
We are whole, never broken, and we are
Swimming in honey-sweet harmony, and
Love – love - loving so endlessly

Because one love guides us,
Our deepest instincts find us, and
Divine love rests inside us, guiding us
Doesn't it feel good?

Compassion

He drove thousands of miles
To go to the funeral -
Grief will make you do that -
Memories enter in and through that.

He cried 'cause he needed the release
And someone to tell him,
"It's okay to stream"
Out our bodies.

He's not a crier - keeps it inside but
He cried gorgeous waterfalls that night and
I held him as he dove in, so
Glad he's been clearer since then.

Light at heart and on his toes
I'm glad to be here for him and
I'm continuing to do so as
We watch over each other.

Light Lives In You

Spinning on a star, forging a path of love
Living a life of absolute abundance
Nothing will fade away, here is where we stay
Here and now is where we stay

Follow your heart; dreams do come true
Never a strife looking back at you
Fly high, hear the angels sing
Open your doors and let yourself ring!

Be kind and true and follow your soul,
Fill up your heart; let it be full
Keep it together, you won't fall apart,
Bound to each other; we're one beating heart

Your heart glows, like the beaming sun
Seek your soul, from it don't run
Dive into your dreams, as dreams do come true
You are the light and the light lives in you

Light Walking

When I'm walking in the sun,
I see things that I've never seen before, and
I see the clouds roll back to the sea
I see a place just for you and for me

When I'm walking in the sun
When I'm thinking of all the good things to come
When I'm chasing clouds from the sky
When I'm living high on love's light

All of the colors of the rainbow swirl together
And in this white ball of love I am spinning
Life could not endure without the light
So I'm singing devotions of delight

When I'm walking in the sun
I see things that I've never seen before
I see the clouds roll back to the sea
I see a place just for you and for me

Into the Light

Journeys through dark always come to the light
Pouring purple paths of insight
Winding and trailing up to the sun
Here is where it was begun

Waiting for the bus in the rain
A neighbor's smile brightens my day
Reminding me of this insight:
Amid loss and strife, we are all light

In blankets cocooning serenity
Floating on love's pleasures,
Sipping on life's serendipity
We share glowing treasures

In light, cornucopias grow bronzed leaves
Red apples & glowing squash
Into life, we twirl away, as
Into the light we run

Connected

Breathing, I'm feeling lighter
Inhaling like a river running through a
Forest; the water is the air trickling,
Flowing into my lungs
Feeding my life, and all life around me

The breath of life fills me up, and I'm
Falling in love with everyone,
Enjoying growing greens and butterflies
Working or cleaning or walking while
Standing on the edge of the balance of life

"It's all good..." pain flows down, above, I rise
To loving this moment so alive, no matter
Interpreting "success" as not a ladder
Opening my lungs to connectedness
Plants, animals, and humans beings

Breathing one breath of conscious
Awareness that we are made of love

Self Love

Choosing to see and hear ourselves on
The inside, finding more and more
Deep within our minds' eye

A journey of thought's thoughts
Seeing peace in love we've got
Run, run, running to grab it

Venturing our causeway, there's a rabbit
Open minds float through the hole
Serenely with the divine we loaf

At the place we live while we dream and
When we're born, of pure sun beams
Conscious now of our glow

Flourishing flora and fauna flow
Seeing everyone in the mirror
Nourishing that which makes us clearer

Love Lights

Golden gleaming sunlight
Finds all the dark spaces and fills them up

Brilliantly beaming, leaves unfurling
Flowers unfolding, touching the light

Softness and fullness, a quenched thirst for berries
Deliciously plump from the sun ripened vine

Richly they beckon us
"Open your eyes!"

Sleepy slumber, awakening wonder
A sunset so full of thunder

Quickly unleash the wandering beast
Run free; we are all free!

Leaves on the breeze, waves upon water
Gently licking the shores evermore

Immersing in beauty of gorgeous things
Life giving water and sunshine on everything

Envisioning Light

I feel love coming and going,
Through and around me,
Flowing all the time, and

I feel the purpose of life,
Like a wave washing over me
Unstoppably

All facets of life are important,
As death takes away,
Life rebirths all that is

Endless cycle of light,
Of the universe, living in me
Emerging

I envision the light
Coming into my heart,
Into my home, into my hearth

I envision the light
Moving through my whole body
Brightening my scene so I'm sparkling

Love

In bugs, frogs, flowers and parrots
Rainbows, sloths, lemurs and carrots
Love lives in us all

In blossoms and berries, petunias and cherries
In glowing mangos and feathery fairies
Love glows from us all

From laughter releasing the stings from the bees
To growing fluttering, shimmering wings
Love shines through us all

Shine

Feel the divinity of love's light
Extending from his body to her body to mine
Coursing through all veins of time
Shining and alive

Feel the soft love light of others
Penetrate our being like a
Happy flood, sharing these blessed
Moments together in sweet love

Glowing alike, all throughout time
Beaming our greatest happiness for life
All the work I do today, I shall dust in glitter
Feed love to my soul and watch it glimmer!

Thank you, Universe, for sweet existence
Soulfully and lustily shining its love prism
To abide and dance through all of us
Shining lights in blissful love

Gems of One Spark

Heavens sing, and so must I
Like a child taking a ride on a star,
Hold on for dear life,
Remember who you are

Precious lovers of God
Light shines through as you sing your song
Lovers, we are all lovers of light,
Solely spinning magical life

Pictures of wholeness, purity, & love
Quenching our thirst with songs from above
Spirits abound, dancing around,
Gems of one spark, igniting the dark

Angels sing through tea green leaves
Brilliantly woven, sister and brother
Love's light, singing with great insight,
Wild, bright, and lusty

Nowland

Sitting, sleeping, breathing, eating
Living in the light, so tender
Sharing crimson sunsets, sprinkling
Rain onto the desert

Bees bestow this alive
Bumble buzzing to their hive
Perpetual love, tangerine poppies
Agape love, newborn puppies

Nature's luscious hedges grow
Misty jade serenity flows
Spirit guides' wands arise
Flooding us all in love vibes

There it grows, feel it expand
Morphing into nurturing Nowland
Breathing softly this inhale
Love demystifies life's sail

Love Listens

Love everlasting; forever abounding
Lighting the paths we are finding

Love uniting and love releasing
Love giving breath to love never ceasing

Singing all day of only Love's Light,
The birds do it; why shouldn't I?

Love sets free, and love delights,
Love is what's keeping us all alive

Speak to me, angels of Love's Light;
Sing soft and ease my sorrowful fright

Shout out so we all hear your words,
"Love lights our way, and we are all heard"

Loving

Two paths lead to the very same place,
No matter if we meditate or pray
When shown the path, it's up to us to lead the way,
Open the door and be amazed.

Spiritual journeys are for discovering,
Heaven's inside us wherever we're hovering
Spiraling on infinite paths of prosperity,
Living this truth and singing life's blessings.

Light upon particle; interpretation
Living and breathing innovation,
Merging through the cosmos' fluorescence,
Floating on a bubble of iridescence.

Seeing value in our dreams,
Truth in fantasy, and
Loving is all that becomes of "We,"
Loving is all that we need.

Perspectives

Light speed
Waves of light dashing
Coursing through and around
Dancing in circular fashion

Spinning and twirling
Billions of waves of light streams
Plateaus of geometric planes
Slower or faster, all happening

Right now, in this moment
Recognizing breathing, in and out
Layers of clear balls of
Threads created from beams of light

Vibrating and crossing paths
Weaving patterns to understand
Pictures in a hologram
Layering perspectives we understand

In one instant to the next
Instant to the next
Instant and so on
And so on

Synergy

Loops and paths, twists and turns
Downs and ups and upside downs

Flowers opening and closing
Vines growing; moving

Tumbling rocks on their own accord
Trembling volcanoes, earthquakes, twisters

Breathing, living, alive, alive
Earth moving, sun grooving,

Everything's flowing light's action
Happening now

(…and now… and now… and now…)

Source is the source is the light, light moving
Breathing, expanding, clear strings connecting

I move left, you move right, dancing
Feeling your thoughts, feeling mine

Rising, falling, pushing and pulling
Forward and backward, glowing in life

Perception

Breathe, refresh, roll your neck
Around in circles, yes it
Feels so good in this moment's
Chance of creating happiness

To bring us all with you as you
Continue to perpetuate life
As light goes on forever and
Continues to multiply

We experience perception of
Different pieces of the same big
Puzzle, and though my piece is my
Own, we all fit into the same picture

Every piece, infinitely born, with
Puzzle upon puzzle thriving
Richly in this universe, only to
Kick back and be examined and

Expanded, as we happily
Hang out in this cosmic vibe,
Enjoying the gift of eternal life
Forever pleasing our love of light

Spirit

At peace in their arms, I rest so completely
Rocked back and forth, whispering

Belief is all I need to be held; comforted,
Embraced, cradled, and loved...

Love, love, love!

A euphoric sensation comes over me -
Joyful tingling touch of spirit;

Living light, love, and perpetual positivity -
You release me

Heaven

Big ball rolling through deep space
Sun shining on us in its grace

A walk by the river when we go camping
Feels so extraordinarily relaxing

Forest fire filling the air with smoke
Makes our eyes burn, makes us choke

A thorn stuck in my foot, juxtaposed
With kissing you passionately on my toes

You handed me a wildflower and I laughed gleefully
Thanks also for the twenty bucks you loaned me

It fell out of my pocket somewhere on the drive
Living in the dark and light at the same time

Infinity is a tiny tip, a teensy-tiny spot
The last drop of tea in my teapot

In this very moment we bring heaven to earth
In this timeless capsule ecstasy is in our birth

Heaven is around us, glowing in the light
Expanding current consciousness all of the time

Winding around and through us, as deep inside
We fill up our cups and let our souls fly

The Love of God

Talk to a chipmunk, marmot, or squirrel
Converse with a dog, cat, boy or a girl
Listen to their stories because everything they say
Has depth and has meaning each and every day

The sun shines on; see the sun shining on?
So we live with this star guiding us along
Yes, the sun shines on and talks through the chatter
Twitters of the birds and hum of gray matter

Listen carefully - who's talking to you?
Is your mind, or the cosmic glue -
Holding us together in this tightly woven pattern,
Brilliant and vibrantly sewn together

Cucumbers soaking in sun, snails on the run
Dolphins jumping, wild and carefree
With joyful love's blessed serenity, and angels
Ticking in our souls, we are the love that we own

We are the love of God

Printed in the United States
By Bookmasters